DRIVE

poems by

Sigrun Susan Lane

Finishing Line Press
Georgetown, Kentucky

DRIVE

ACKNOWLEDGMENTS

Grateful acknowledgment is made to the editors of the following publications where these poems, some of which have been subsequently revised, originally appeared:

Arnazella: "Bride and Groom"
Poet's West: "Heaven is Being a Memory to Others"
Raw Art Review: "The Remington" and "Sunday Drive With Daddy in Hunting Season"
Seattle Review: "Looking for Amelia" and "My Father's Story"
Green Silk Journal: "The Dancer"
Young Ravens: "When Mother Took Her hair Down"
Montana Mouthful: "Road Test"
Asheville Poetry Review: "Venison"
Halfway Down the Stairs: "The Botanist"

Publisher: Leah Huete de Maines
Editor: Christen Kincaid
Cover Art: topseller // Shutterstock
Author Photo: D. Fontana
Cover Design: Elizabeth Maines McCleavy

Order online: www.finishinglinepress.com
also available on amazon.com

Author inquiries and mail orders:
Finishing Line Press
PO Box 1626
Georgetown, Kentucky 40324
USA

Contents

Looking at My Father 1

Driving with Daddy 2

The Dancer 3

Bride and Groom 4

When the Fleet Came Home 5

USS Osprey 6

Wild Animals 7

Stolen Swim 8

The Remington 9

When Mother Took Her Hair Down 10

Brownie Hawkeye 12

The Big Winner 13

The Road Test 14

The Voles 15

Orange Cessna 16

Daddy Takes the Oldsmobile Over Colockum Pass, 1964 17

Out of High Country 18

Sunday Drive with Daddy in Hunting Season 19

Venison 20

Jackpot 21

My Father Teaches Me to Fish 22

Out of Vegas 23

The Botanist 24

Homecoming 25

The Crash 26

His Ring 27

Looking for Amelia 28

The Grey Wolf 29

My Father's Story 30

Heaven is Being a Memory to Others 31

My Father's War 32

Looking at My Father

When I was a child I never tired of looking at my father.
I could not get enough of the large hall of his forehead,
his black hair and widow's peak, dark brows,
his eyes, irises glittering toward black.
A hunter's eyes. The whites
lightly stained, lashes like thickets.
From his spot on the plane
he took in everything—
the landscape, position of targets,
landing decks on carriers at sea.
His nose straight.
His mouth neither full nor flat,
filled with talk, lies and stories, blinding curses.
His locker held uniforms;
summer whites, winter blues,
gold stripes on the sleeves.
Dressed to fly in a leather flight jacket
white parachute silk at his neck—
I would gaze in adoration.
Sometimes during air raid blackouts
he would cradle me,
dance music playing in the dark,
the radio's bright eye covered.
I liked the size of him—
the biggest thing in our house.
And the most dangerous.

Driving with Daddy

He liked his cars big, he liked them fast,
V-8 engines, power steering, chrome-loaded
Oldsmobiles, Buicks and Cadillacs.

He was always going somewhere else,
he was restless like that.
Daddy drove us all over "God's Country".

We knew we were in California
when we woke to see luminous oranges
like myriad small suns clinging to the trees.

He flew us through a thousand tiny towns.
Their names a blur, Red Lodge Ennis Tombstone
to Indian War battlefields—

Rosebud, Little Bighorn, Bear Paw.
Guarded by ghosts, their voices
we heard wailing in the wind.

Wild horses grazed in the low lands.
Startled antelope leapt, white tails in the air.
When dark-faced buffalo stared at us, we stared back.

We traversed Death Valley in winter,
so cold at night,
our pee froze solid on the highway.

Then the Yellowstone crater with its fissures
and fumaroles, where the earth's heat leaks out.
A golden angel trumpeted on a temple top.

When the Cessna crashed and he was gone,
we slashed the front tires on the Buick,
to make sure his car stayed in the driveway.

The Dancer
—after Geoffrey Davis

In Seattle, in 1932, my mother beholds this man
across a dance floor, the one she's already

turning into my father. He's a dancer.
Handsome in his natty sailor blues,

thirteen buttons on the front of his bell bottoms,
a flap on the back of his jumper,

knotted tie, the full regalia.
That smile. Her heart yawns open

to let him in. He glides toward her
shy smiling face. She waits

eager to be asked. And they dance,
because they are born to it—foxtrot, lindy hop,

their bodies finding new ways to move.
They dance because the night must not end,

morning must never come, the band must play forever,
this must be their lives, dancing in each other's arms,

with rain falling outside on the grey city,
the windows wet and weeping.

My mother would never blame him
or that smile for all that happened.

All those years after, she learned to forgive
him for his long absences. For better, for worse,

was all that mattered. No matter what others said.
She chose him, again and again. That smile.

Bride and Groom

They must have stood on the Depression
wedding cake up to their ankles in icing,
their little bodies bent together,
embracing. He's in a top hat and tux,
she's in a long gown and toque.
Although they are well over fifty,
they are still clinging.
I want to ask these little China heads,
Did the bride dance? Was the groom laughing?
Were their faces as bland and lovely as yours?

I know what they cannot know:
how they will make of their marriage
a thirty-years war: how their children
will run from their burning house.
I want to help the little bride to climb
down the steep slopes, to find a way out
among the pink rosettes.
I want the groom to glissade
from the summit, top hat and all,
a small dark figure against the snowy cake.

I want to tell them *no*.
Instead the figures slip from my hands
crash in pieces on the floor
and I am on my knees among the shards
Sifting and fitting, her foot, his head.
I glue them back together again
so their lives will reel out,
where I wait to wiggle into life.
This story begins with memory:
Sharp, urgent splinters of clay.

When the Fleet Came Home

When the great grey ships sailed in, our mothers
put on lipstick, curled their hair.
Beer chilled, parties broke out, dance music flared

into the night. The Dorsey Brothers' band
played *Red Sails in the Sunset.* Our dads
circled our mothers in clumsy dance steps.

These men were like strange noisy animals,
muscled and sun-tanned. They smelled
of beer and sweat, took up space in back yards

and living rooms which they filled
with talk, cigarette smoke and jokey laughter.
Their white tee shirts glowed in the sun.

They slid effortlessly to the head
of the table, behind the wheel of the car.
Their voices rose over all the others.

They shouted to each other, shouted at us,
as we ran between the houses.
Dusk at a volleyball net, the men leapt

into the darkening night like pale birds flying up.
Our mothers watched from the sidelines,
crossing and uncrossing their long, tan legs.

USS Osprey
—U.S. Navy Station, Jacksonville, Florida

On the ship, Daddy puts me in the arms of Curly, my first love.
He carries me along the *Osprey's* clanging metal compartments,

her ominous corridors, past numbered battle stations to the bridge.
My greedy eyes spy a ration of candy from a seaman's horde.

I am five years old, all curls and ruffles,
my fingers sticky with Cracker Jacks.

Homesick deckhands look up from their work,
take a break from scrape and paint.

They come in faded blue dungarees, sailor hats tipped back,
they come laughing, grabbing a smoke on the way.

Today I am the darling of every man onboard,
A sailor shows me a picture of his daughter. Blonde like me.

One man plants his hat on my head. Parades me
around the deck, humming "Sweet Sue".

The sun beats hard on our heads. From my perch on a gun turret,
the metal glows hot through my cotton underpants.

Wild Animals

We lived with ibex, leopards,
wildebeests, bush books, a kudu.
A sable in the kitchen.
In the hall, a caracal.
We moved out—
while we were gone, the animals moved in.
Our home, a kind of mausoleum.
The mounted beasts cast shadows on our play.
Glass eyes stared into dead space,
to places we couldn't see.
We ran below their great furred heads.
No matter how loud we screamed,
they didn't blink.
Horns spiked the air,
like a bad dream in daylight.
Dad's friend Bruce killed them all.
I didn't like to think about their deaths
in the heat of an African afternoon,
the sound the leopard made when she dropped.
And the wildebeest. Bullet to the brain.
In the dark they padded upstairs to my room,
filled my head with visions of the savanna.
They dwelled a year or so with us,
then the trophy hunter trucked them off.
Their heads imprinted on the walls,
like ghosts, their stubborn hunger.

Stolen Swim

"*When the whole world is water, there is nothing to do but swim in the rain.*"

We steal across the grounds of a brick mansion,
three teenage girls on a lark.
Cool June in the rain, the sky low and grey.
Through a picture window the man
of the house sits in a green chair,
in a circle of lamp light reading the Times.
He holds the paper out-stretched in front of him,
one tan pant leg crossed over the other,
a dark brown sweater, gold-rimmed glasses.

We had not counted on finding someone home.
Out teenage brains decide this is a risk
worth taking. We strip.
Cold air goose bumps our naked flesh.
We move to the pool, slide into warm water.
Stifle our delight. Look up at the the man
in the brown sweater. He carefully turns a page.

If he looks out the window he would see us
swim like young dolphins
in his pool. See our bodies delight
in the dimpling water, rain running
in rivulets down our faces, our skin.
He would watch us play
like young seals, over and under the water.
His eyes would notice the pleasure
we take in our bodies, their slipperiness—
how they glide through water.
If he looks up, he would see bare breasts
float like islands, nipples perk
in cool air, his pool filling with pale breasts
and bottoms, bottoms and breasts rising
and falling in the downpour. The rain tendering
every part of us which is after all, what we seek.

The Remington

In his blackest rages the Remington
came out of the closet.
He held it in his right hand, pointed it
at his head, as he paced and howled
into dark and sleepless hours.
The Remington lived like a snake
in the front closet behind the coats.
Sometimes I opened the closet just to look
where it stood, straight up in the corner,
wooden stock, steel barrel.
Always there waiting.
I never knew when it would come out,
fill our house with its sorrow, its smell.
Like a snake's lair. That stench.

When Mother Took Her Hair Down

When Mother took her hair down
in order to wash it, we gathered round
to see it fall nearly to her knees—

the strangeness of it.
She was an ancient sorceress,
her hair fell in wondrous waves.

We imagined what could live there
in the dark curtains, small animals,
fairies perhaps, ladders for little people

who built homes in her tresses.
We played peek boo through its drapery
until she shooed us, so she could wash it.

She sat before the fireplace to dry
it, bent forward so it cascaded.
We could see the fire through it

as she brushed. We huddled
close to her feet for warmth.
She brushed and brushed.

We asked to help, but our small hands
did not have the strength
to handle its thickness, its body.

Then she gathered it up and braided
in that funny way of hers.
She held a strand in her mouth,

fixed two thick braids then wound them
round in the style of her Icelandic mother.
She looked old fashioned and regal,

like a visitor from a faraway country
where nature is cruel
and a woman is prized for the hair on her head.

My New Brownie Hawkeye

I stand with my best friend
on the barren bluff by our new home.
The ground beneath us, hard-packed and weedy.
We are ten years old. My blonde hair, an uproar of curls,

We will take our own photos—
not the pictures our parents take of us,
where we smile on command,
squinting into the sun.

See how we pose:
Nancy, the stepchild, in her sagging socks
and worn out shoes looks straight ahead.
I angle my feet like the models in magazines.

I stand tall in my white blouse,
sandals and white anklets.
Look straight into the Hawkeye.
The camera sees me as I am,

and as I wish to be seen—
a girl who will not stay long
in this place, a girl with plans for herself.
A picture of a girl going places.

The Big Winner

Pit bosses bowed as he passed,
gamblers reached out to touch him for luck.
I watched as Dad came to get me
from the Teen lounge, two tall hookers
attached to his arms, he dusted off like horseflies.
His pockets bulged with chips.
He took me with him to the Cashiers' window,
where he lined up the chips by value;
so many columns, so many rows,
exchanged for hundreds of Franklin's faces.
Bills flashed into a fan, then fanned into a stack.
Some to his boot, some to his wallet.
All that money, just like that.
We drove into the desert dark past dazzling neon,
white trumpeting fountains, to one of the Strip's
ritzy all-night boutiques where it was three o'clock
in the morning and always mid-day.
Mom and the kids asleep at the motel.
"Get your mother something nice," he said.
Nothing in Las Vegas was anything like my mother.

Road Test

Here we go again,
flying across the desert,
Mother in the front seat with her silent prayers;
Dad guns the engine of the new Buick.
The small towns a blur.
A two-lane highway across an immense landscape.
Like the flat bottom of a great sea, he tells us.
This was once an ocean teeming with life,
amazing sea creatures.
I can almost see it in the washed-out land.
Everywhere there is sand.
If I close my eyes, I can flood
this great basin, see the bony fish,
giant squid swimming in the depths.
Somewhere farther out they are
testing bombs, a burst of light,
a large mushroom cloud rises
into heaven, signaling the gods
we have such power.
Melted the eyes of those
too close to the flash.
Atomic bombs. That can end all life.
They don't count this land for much,
or the people who live on it—
a land steeped in loneliness
and hard to love,
the bow-tied men far away
grinding out reports.

The Vole

All night I dreamed of *voles*—
the word, the soft velvet sound of it
burrowed into my dreams,
a single syllable, soft and furry.
I never held one,
those pocket-sized creatures,
like a mouse.
They lived in the sands of the Mojave,
on Area 51, the blast area
for nuclear testing of the '50's.
They tunnel in the sands,
set up families underground,
come up to test the air
like a prairie dog.
I know its cousin,
the mole, have cursed it
as it laid waste to my garden
with its small pink hands, hooded eyes.
And the vole, is just as dread
to the farmer, because of its immense
appetite for roots and grain.
The one I dreamed dug deep
into its earthen cave with its offspring,
was vaporized along with the snakes,
the Side-blotched lizards, the Prairie dogs,
the Kangaroo rats, the Gila monsters,
the Pocket mice, the Jack rabbits,
the Burrowing Owls and the Roadrunners
when the A-bomb burst over them.

The Orange Cessna

Today we have the sky to ourselves—
immense, faultless and blue.
We head over the Sound, the islands
below us, deep green water lilies.

At altitude, he flies air-show maneuvers—
barrel rolls. Fast, like a roller coaster.
We rush up one side upside down,
held by our seat belts, then down.

Clutching the edge of my seat,
heart hammering, dry mouthed,
I glance at my dad. Flying kindles
a light in him. His eyes shine.

He has always been turned on by speed—
fast cars or racing boats,
by the close whisper of death, the way
some people love to start fires

or balance on a wire strung high
between buildings. It's part of him
like his black hair and brown eyes.
Now he points the nose straight up,

we climb a vertical wall of air.
The engine coughs, stalls out.
The plane hangs for a moment in silence.
He points the Cessna down in a nosedive—

we do this over and over.
Dad laughs in the open face of the sky.
He doesn't care if I am frightened.
He's not that kind of dad.

Daddy Takes the Oldsmobile Over Colockum Pass, 1964
—see Kittitas County Map and Trail Guide

He sees dotted lines on the map
to find this twisted way.
We jostle and jolt up a steep slope

along a track dug deep in on the sides,
high in the middle.
The engine grinding, he shifts into low gear,

hunches over the wheel, keen and alert.
Now just the heave ho of the car,
as it lurches, high centers on the stiff dirt track.

Tree branches scrape the sides of the car.
When the Olds noses over the top of the pass,
we scatter sheep grazing among the pines,

startle three Basque shepherds.
We have motored in from another time,
another country.

We stumble from the car,
our feet uncertain in the hummocks
and jumble of the road,

breathe in the piney air,
speak a few words in Spanish,
to the men who stare and do not speak.

We do not understand
our presence here,
where we are going or why.

We gaze out at mountains
rising blue grey like
hump backed whales.

Out of High Country

Basque shepherds nod a silent good bye,
happy to be done with us.
We set out down a single track,

dug in deep on both sides, high in the middle.
Each jolt throws us forward, out of our seats.
Pine branches scratch at the windows.

Dirt and rock scrape the underbelly
loosen bolts, sheer couplings.
Dad's hands tighten on the wheel.

Scored steel screeches in a high metal voice,
like a human cry we can't help.
We count how far we've come,

how far to go. Have no idea.
To each their own calculation.
We worry the radiator.

Downward we wind for hours,
mumbled conversation.
Finally, the river valley,

where the Yakima River opens space
for sky and a highway,
smooth and flat.

Near nightfall great coulees rise around us
like sleeping goliaths.
We coast into Coulee City,

the Olds dragging its pipes on the road,
sparks fly—a rooster tail flares in the dark.
Dad leaves the Olds in a used car lot.

Sunday Drive with Daddy in Hunting Season

Deer season the Remington lay across Daddy's lap,
Mom next to him in the front, the five of us kids in the back.
We drove the high country on logging roads.
He hunted from his '56 Cadillac, the green one
with leopard skin upholstery, dual pipes.
We climbed the rough dirt track through tall timber.
With one hand on the steering wheel,
his window rolled down, he scanned the woods for antlers,
for any movement in the brush.
Shushed to silence lest we spook the game,
we huddled low in the back seat.
I prayed for the deer hidden in the underbrush.
I could think only of the menace of the gun
lying there, loaded at the ready.
In the deep quiet of the forest,
the car's deep rumble.

Venison

When I saw him, the deer was roped
to the hood of the car.
The slender head rested there.
Flies gathered at the glazed eyes,
at the corners of the mouth.
He had a fine brace of antlers,
dark bones branched like birch trees.
I searched to find the places
where the bullets entered,
where the dark flew in, his spirit flew out—
Small holes, the fur around them stiff with blood.
I patted the deer, as if to comfort him.
The pelt thick and rough where I touched.
Soon he will be split, haunches from sternum,
then dressed with a knife.
The knife will slice abdomen
and rectum, will slide through fascia,
split buttock from leg, muscle from bone.
Wrapped in brown paper and frozen,
food we will consume all year.
Without ceremony,
we will gather around the table.
I will eat the wild meat,
and slowly it will become my own body.

Jackpot

That time Dad hit a big jackpot,
gamblers bent three deep around the table,
they pressed in to touch his sleeves,
they wanted to catch his luck like a cold.

Hookers swarmed him like honeybees
and he was an orange blossom.
The room sang with the sound of payoffs
from glowing machines.

That night we dined late, he got up early to buy
a green Cadillac, the color of money.
He sped across the desert, doing over a hundred
when we were pulled over.

He got a ticket from a cop looking
for big winners speeding out of town in big cars.
I can still see that cop's face,
his amber sunglasses glinting in the sun.

My Father Teaches Me to Fish

I watched him thread the herring on the line,
a trick of his made the silver herring dance
as as we mooched for salmon off Point No Point.
Dad played out a lot of line. When a salmon
takes the bait it runs deep. And heavy gauge;
it can snap thin filament. Things my dad knew.
I was eight years old, had a rod too.
Watched the tip for a quiver, for a strike.
I was ready with a hook and a net to boat the fish,
lay it flopping on the deck. A blow to the head.
An end to suffering.
Dad taught me how to gut a fish—
up through the bung hole to the gills.
To pee in a Folger's can. Life's necessary skills.

Out of Vegas

We burn across a desert flat as a crap table,
sage and tumble weed flying by for miles.
Finally dark, stars catch fire one by one,
glow all the way to Reno.

In the motel, silently without seeming too,
I pray he will find his way back to winning,
to his chosen vocation, that singular calling,
that split second before the dice tumble and fall.

The Botanist

From the bus my mother
bird-walked narrow planting strips,
green Eden of wildness,

bent to pick weeds--
stalk, root and flowers,
to be pressed between waxed paper,

named from Ada Georgia's *Manual of Weeds*.
Each specimen labeled; its seed splayed.
She called them by their common names

and by their Latinate,
meadow buttercup, *Ranunculus acris,*
common chickweed, *Stellaria media,*

yarrow, *Achillea millefollium*
and mother's heart, *Capsella bursa-pastoris*
which grows everywhere.

Mother knew that every part
of the dandelion, the stinging nettle's
stem and bloom, red buttons

of the salmonberries
were food, *makamaka,*
for the Chinook tribes.

Believed that plants like people
have hidden virtues, this
is what she loved in them.

She wandered farther afield,
returned, her face flushed, hat askew,
a clutch of bane in her hands.

Homecoming

That night when he was at last home,
the talk of the joint still stuck in his speech.
The doorbell's benediction rang over the heads

of strangers. Men who stopped, but did not stay.
Shook his hand, mumbled quick conversations.
One handed off a bottle of whiskey.

He moved slowly through the house,
as if blind. Reclaimed his home by touch.
Handled the doors. Stroked

the frayed furniture, its nubs and wrinkles,
moved room to room,
slid his fingers over each worn thing,

remembering— the scarred dining table,
thick nap of towels.
Each picture-framed face.

Then he sat down in his chair,
that still held his body's shape,
looked up to see the faces of his children.

These children grown tall in his absence.
They looked at him, tried to understand
what had gone so wrong in his life—

what would become of him now—
and of them, still living
under the roof beams of the old house.

The Crash

I think he meant to set the plane in the treetops
once he knew he was off course,

once the fog broke clear and he could see the mountain,
the dense stand of Douglass fir looming straight ahead.

I think he tried to decelerate, to land the Cessna
in the smaller tree tops that hot July afternoon.

I believe my dad "flew the plane down".
That's what seasoned pilots do.

Two people on the right-hand side of the plane
lived through the crash.

Mom's last words were his name.
"Bob," she said, "Bob."

But what do I know?
I wasn't there. I am only a survivor.

His Ring

Let me not forget the shiny zircon
he wore on his little finger like a diamond.
It flashed like his smile. Showed him
to be a player,

a man of substance.

I like to think about the Swiss bank account. He said
the money is in a numbered account
in Switzerland. There for the taking,
if you know the number.

What's the damn number?

His ring is missing.
Someone must have stripped it from his finger.
I'm told that happens at crash sites. Watches, rings.
All the bright and shiny things,

everything goes.

Looking for Amelia

I was not alive when my father went looking
for Amelia Earhart those long months
in the interminable Pacific, steaming island
to island in 1939, where it is getting late.
He charted as he ran, drawing
fine grey lines to mark beachheads,
circling coral reefs with coffee stains.

He reckoned latitude and longitude,
measured and mapped each islet
as if it were somewhere,
sounded league after league
of mountain ranges and vast plains
lying fathoms below.

Months at sea, the ocean
stretched taut as a drum.
The equatorial days cloudless
as a night without dreams.
No sign of Amelia, only the soft ping
of the sonar, the throb of engines
spinning a trail of lacy phosphorus.
At night the bridge glowed red,
The vision of a pale woman
floated above the compass rose.

I too have searched for Amelia,
followed the woman with the brisk walk,
the jaunty jodhpurs. In the picture
she balances on the flat of a wing,
grinning at the camera, her job just begun.
She turns to wave at us.
Fifty years later I still look for her,
I see her picture everywhere.
I still wave back.

The Grey Wolf

The grey wolf comes loping
over the flat Lutheran landscape of Ballard.
He is spindle-legged—
his work is hard among the restless,
sleepless old Scandinavians
who count their hours in coffee cups,
their mouths stiff and dry as *hardfiskur*.
He is coming for Umma.
She watches for His Narrowness.
Her gnarled hands catch at the window lace,
her face a roadmap of all her journeys.
She has fought many wolves—
driven them from the door
in a rain of Icelandic curses.
The blue-eyed wolf will sit in the parlor,
(where no dog has ever been).
They will sip coffee from a saucer
through a hard sugar cube.
Then he will lie down in a circle of fur
at her feet and they will sleep.

My Father's Story

Father, even in my dreams
you are speeding
driving cars too fast
on roads too narrow.
This morning you streaked
through my just waking
dream and slamming brakes
mouthed silent syllables
behind the driver's window
car rumbling, impatient.
What was it you wanted?

Like the time you dive-bombed
our boat as we drifted miles from land,
from home. Still noon shattered
by a small Cessna roaring
twenty feet overhead
salt shining the windows
you grinning in the cockpit,
winging loop-the-loops over the bow,
my heart pounding fear.
What was it you wanted?

Do you read me, *Whiskey, Zulu, Bravo?*
Over. The air white with silence, static.
Whiskey, Zulu, Bravo, over and over.
A mantra, a prayer for your passage,
the orange plane in memory
a distant fading semaphore.

Heaven is Being a Memory to Others

At the edge of light
       two figures in a boat
and I think I hear your name
said out loud and everywhere you are
(I believe you are everywhere now)
lights up a different goldish color,
and everything hovers and hums—
       the sky pink
       as spun sugar,
the water opals firing pale green
surges in the underwave.
       Now there is nothing
that is not you,
and nothing that is not our inheritance.
       This is the wonder:
when there is no one,
that we live and just when we forget how,
       we remember.

My Father's War

This is how I like to imagine his war—
Dad descending out of the chaos
and smoke of war from a B-29
to some no-name atoll to find my uncle Pete,
a Navy Seabee in the South Pacific in 1943.
Dad has schmoozed his way onto this flight.
He comes out of the tropical blue sky
and sifting clouds like the angel Gabriel.
The landing is bumpy and hard.
Marines only just took this atoll.
Snipers are still firing from the hills,
Seabees are just now finishing the landing strip.
Somehow, he has tracked Pete to this spot,
from hundreds of atolls, from thousands of Seabees.

Pete stands with a work gang,
a truck passes, stirring up red dust.
The sun burns down hot, skin reddens
like the dust. Shade sifts
from the palms that clatter overhead.
Pete can't trust his vision—
a young lieutenant in khaki walks
toward him, calling his name.
The man waves and grins,
he carries a metal briefcase.
This can't be, Pete thinks, *in this god-forsaken
place 3000 miles from nowhere.*
The two men embrace—there is not much time,
the plane revs up on the dirt runway.

This is a year before Pete falls into the hold of a ship,
breaks his back, contracts tuberculosis
in a field hospital in the Pacific.
This is two years before the A-Bomb drops on Hiroshima,
four years before my dad is lured into the notion of free
post-war goods from the Navy base—
before the blame and retribution,
before it all blows up in his face.
Dad opens the metal briefcase.
There is a bottle of good whiskey,
smoked salmon and homemade pickled herring.
Let me leave them on the runway, laughing.

Sigrun Susan Lane is the author of two chapbooks, *Little Bones* and *Salt*, which won the Josephine Miles's award in 2020 from Pen Oakland for excellence in literature. She is a graduate of the University of Washington where she studied Creative Writing, but subsequently pursued a career in business. She returned to writing after a long hiatus.

Her poems have appeared in national and international journals, including *Asheville Poetry Review, Crab Creek Review, Malahat Review, Sing Heavenly Muse* and numerous others. She has won awards for her poetry from the King County Arts and Seattle Arts Commissions.

She lives in Seattle with her husband. She serves as a docent for the Frye Art Museum.